# HOW TO DRAW
## CUTE THINGS BOOK
## FOR KIDS

# This Book Belongs To:

---------------------------------------

---------------------------------------

2

# TABLE OF CONTENTS

# ICE CREAM

# PRACTICE HERE!

# CUPCAKE

# PRACTICE HERE!

# HOUSE

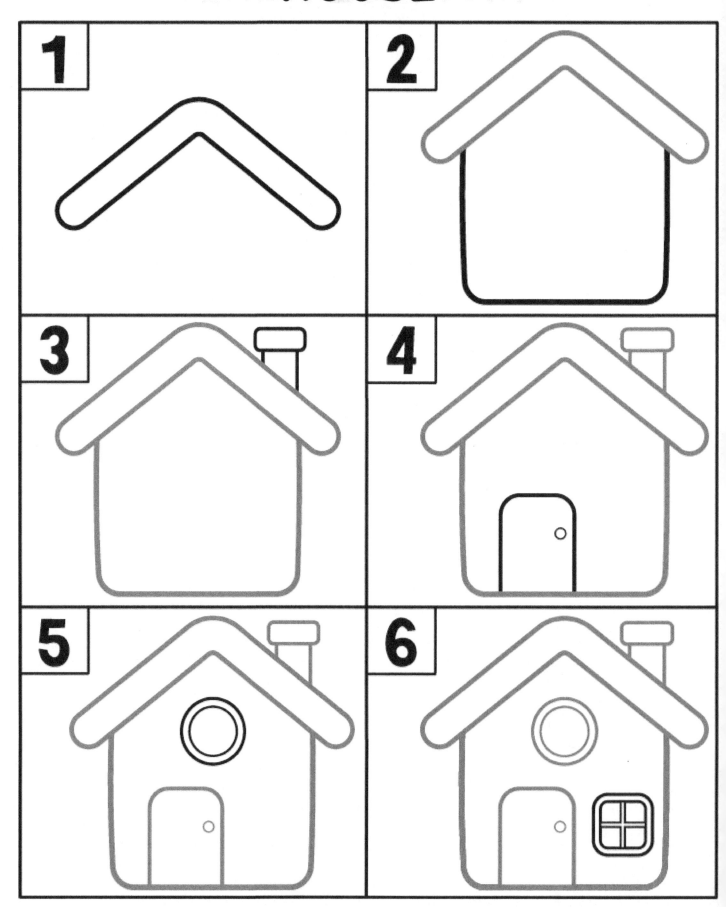

# PRACTICE HERE!

# MUSHROOM

# PRACTICE HERE!

# PIG

# PRACTICE HERE!

# ROBOT

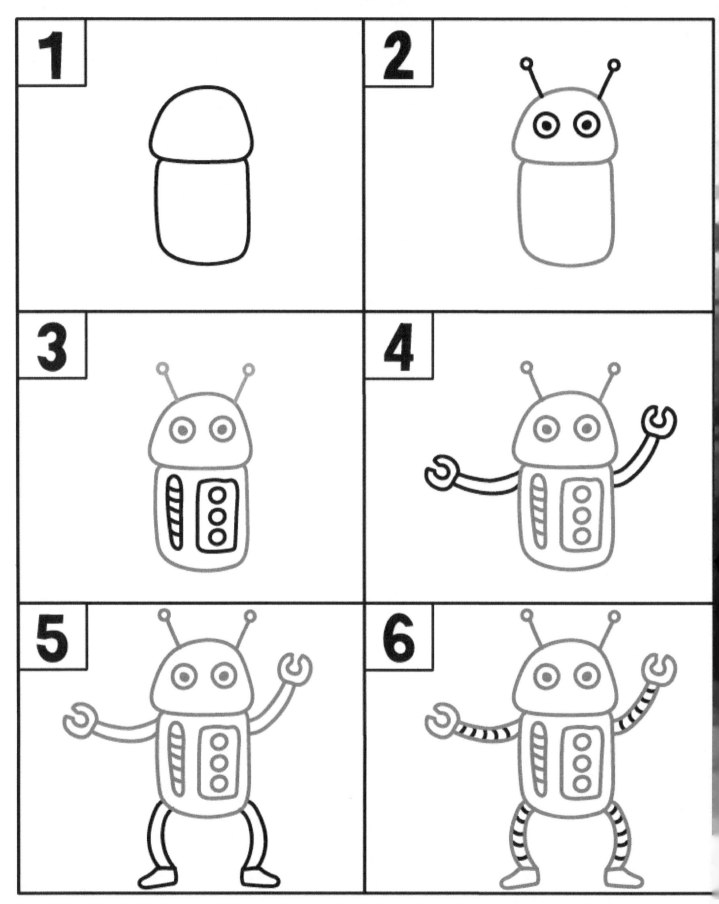

# PRACTICE HERE!

# CAR

# PRACTICE HERE!

# CACTUS

# PRACTICE HERE!

# BIRD

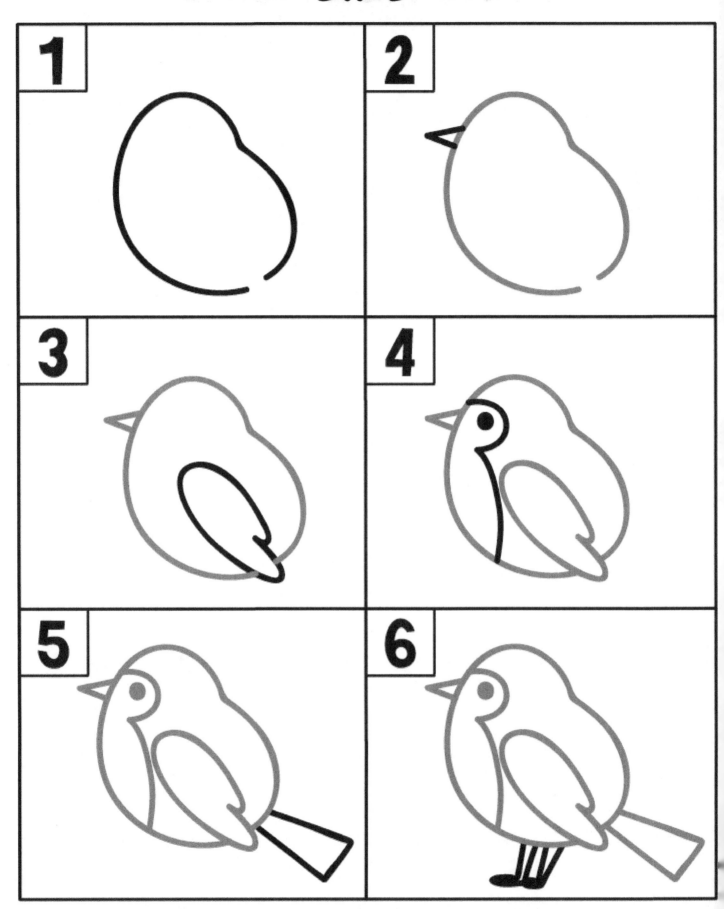

# PRACTICE HERE!

# PIZZA

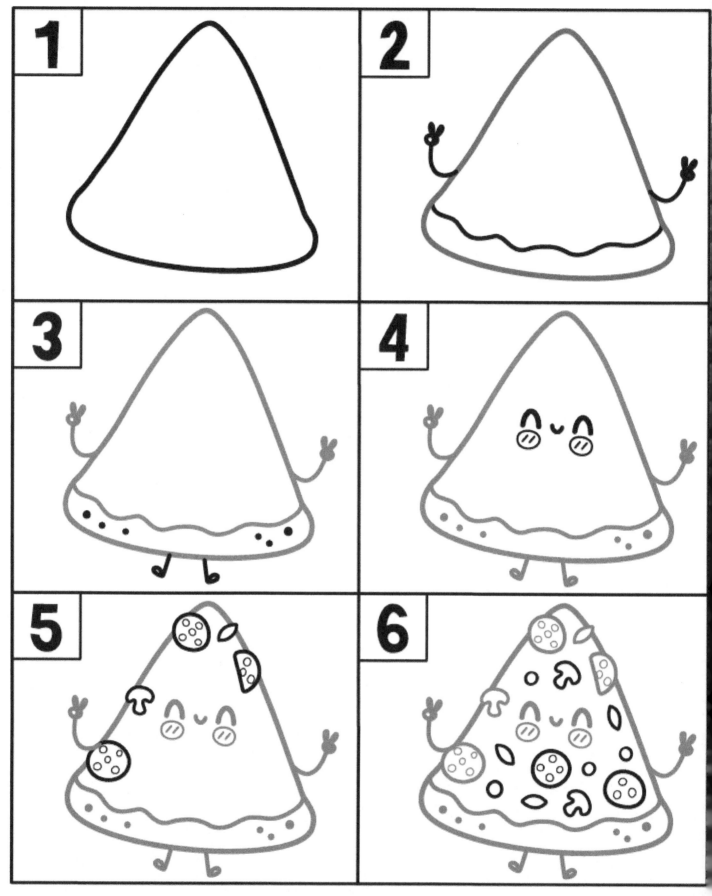

# PRACTICE HERE!

# DONUT

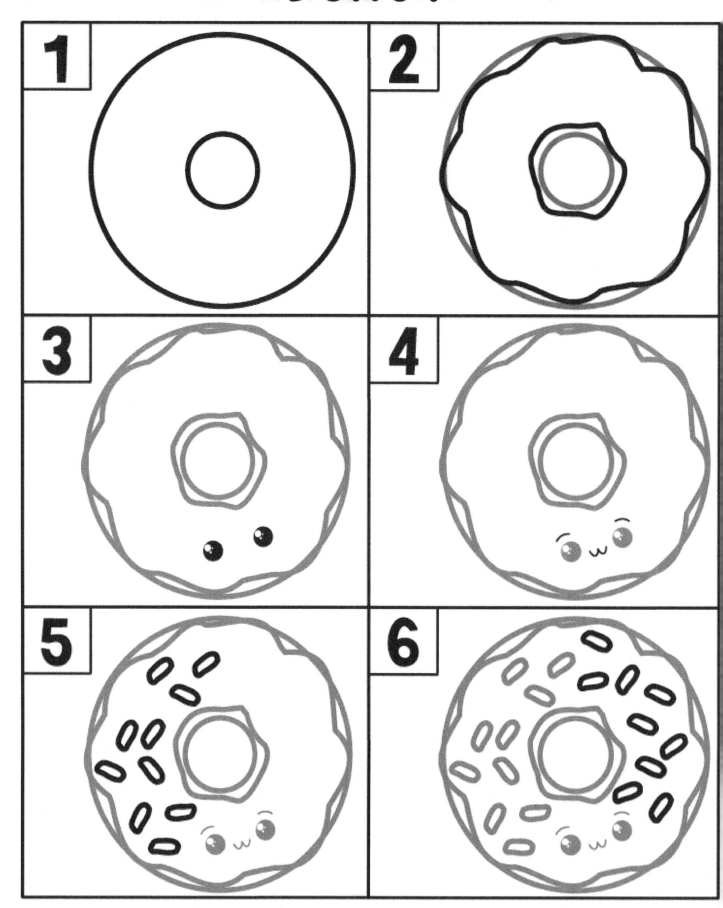

# PRACTICE HERE!

# BEE

# PRACTICE HERE!

# BROCCOLI

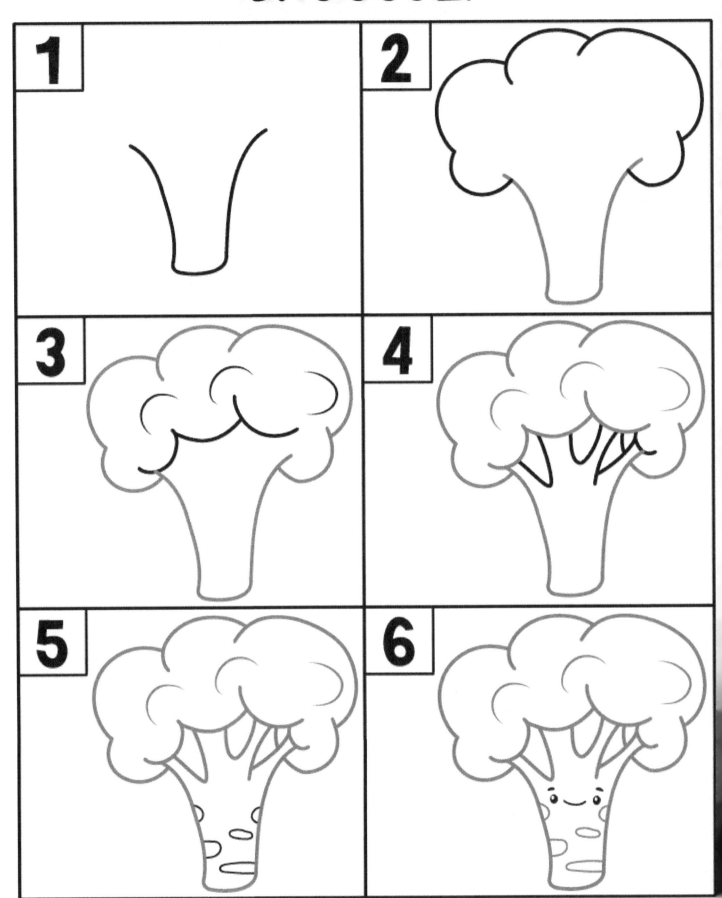

# PRACTICE HERE!

# CRAB

# PRACTICE HERE!

# FLOWER

# PRACTICE HERE!

# FROG

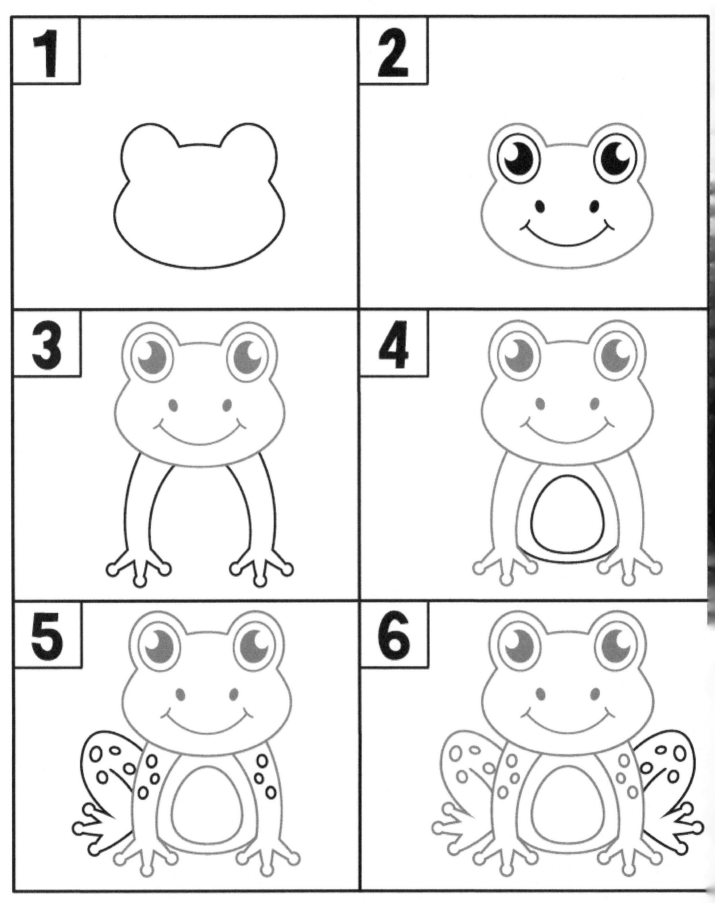

# PRACTICE HERE!

# STRAWBERRY

# PRACTICE HERE!

# MOUSE

# PRACTICE HERE!

# OWL

# PRACTICE HERE!

# PANDA

# PRACTICE HERE!

# BEAR

# PRACTICE HERE!

# MONSTER

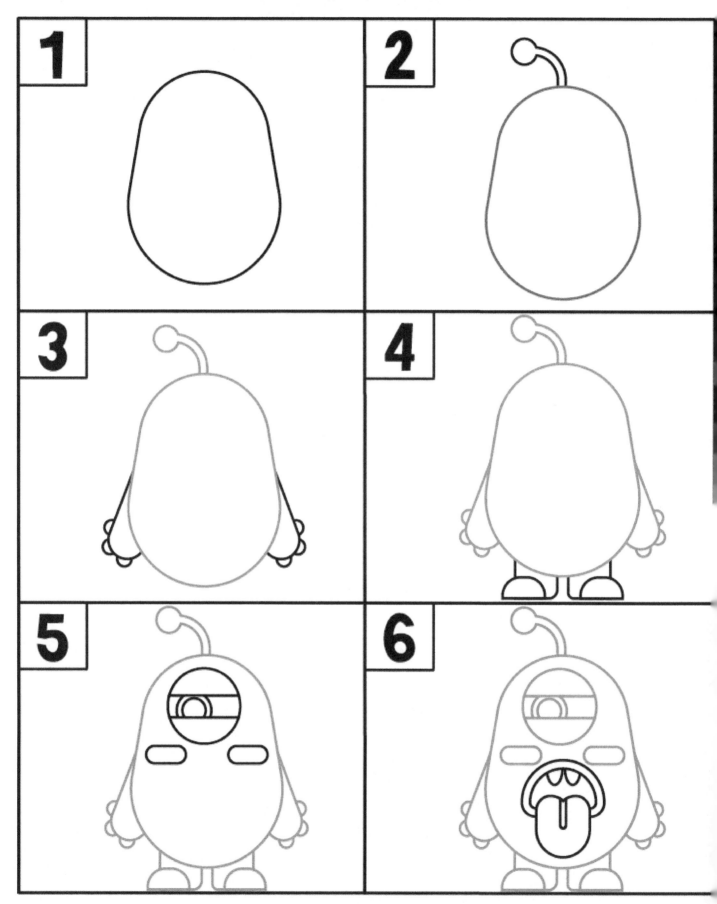

# PRACTICE HERE!

# UNICORN

# PRACTICE HERE!

# BABY DINOSAUR

# PRACTICE HERE!

# PENGUIN

# PRACTICE HERE!

# FISH

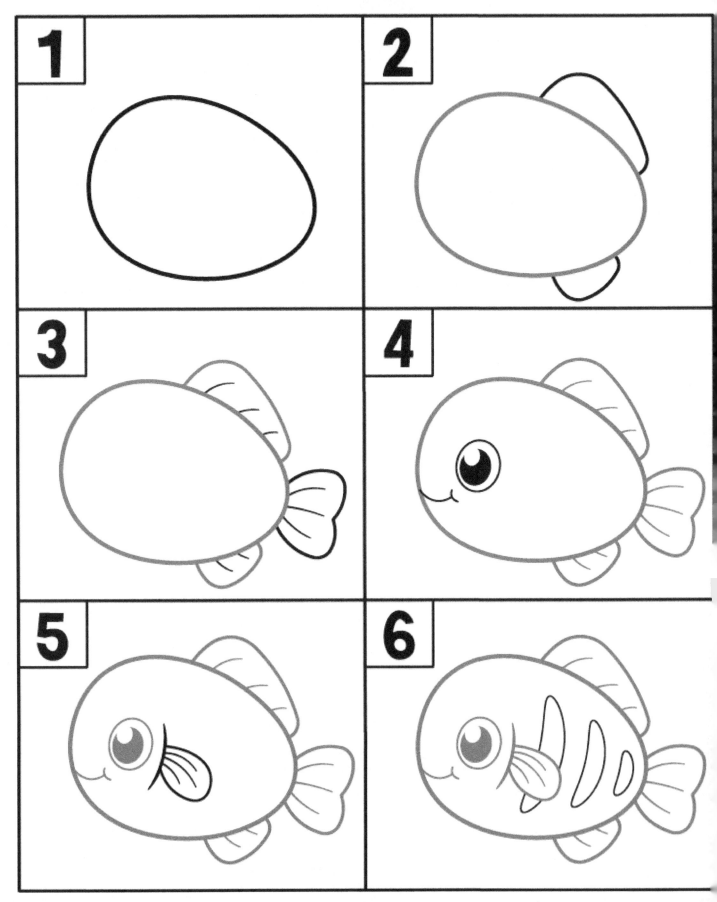

# PRACTICE HERE!

# DOG

# PRACTICE HERE!

# CAT

# PRACTICE HERE!

# BABY DUCK

**1**

**2**

**3**

**4**

**5**

**6**

# PRACTICE HERE!

# OCTOPUS

# PRACTICE HERE!

# POPCORN

# PRACTICE HERE!

# DOLPHIN

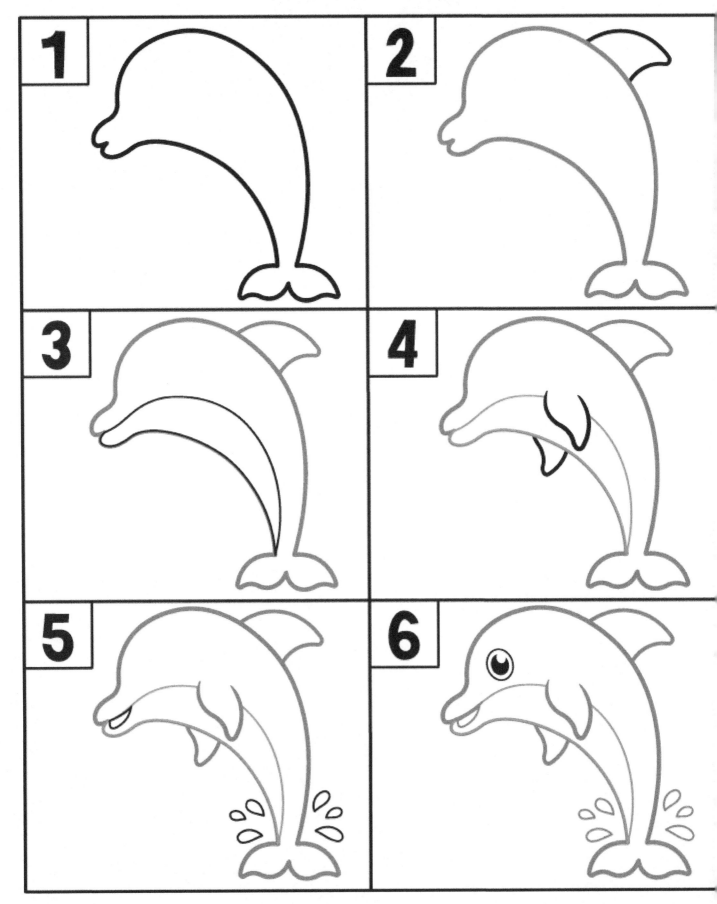

# PRACTICE HERE!

# MILK

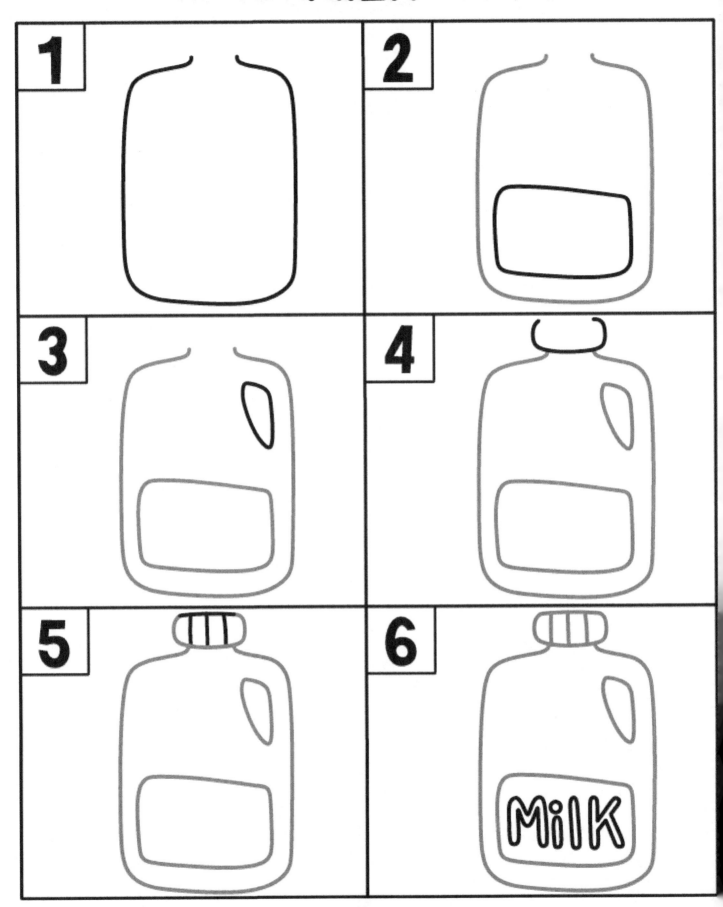

# PRACTICE HERE!

# COOKIES

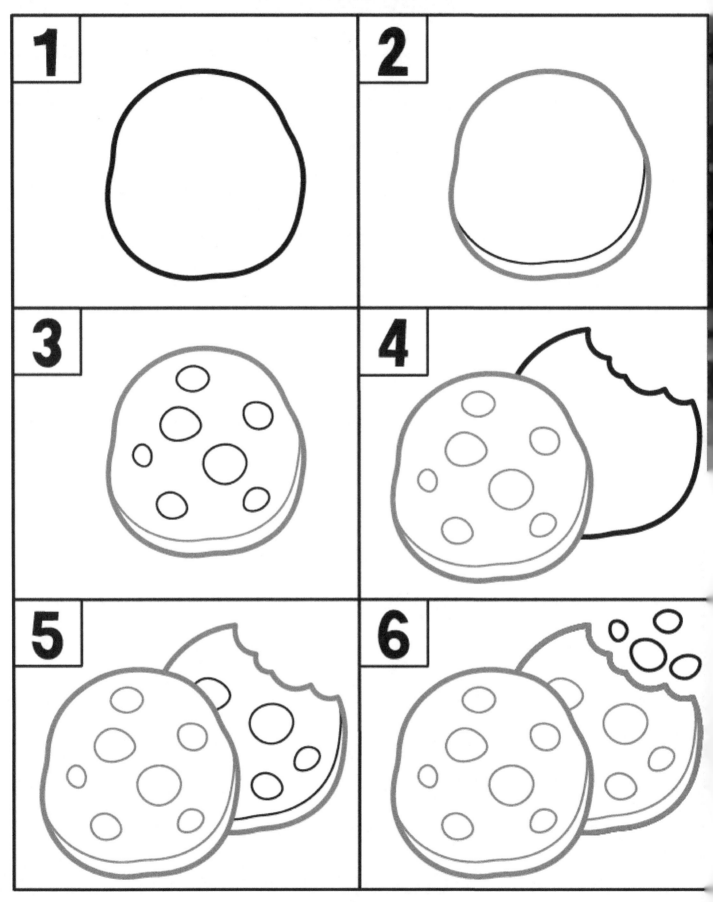

# PRACTICE HERE!

# EGG

# PRACTICE HERE!

# TOAST

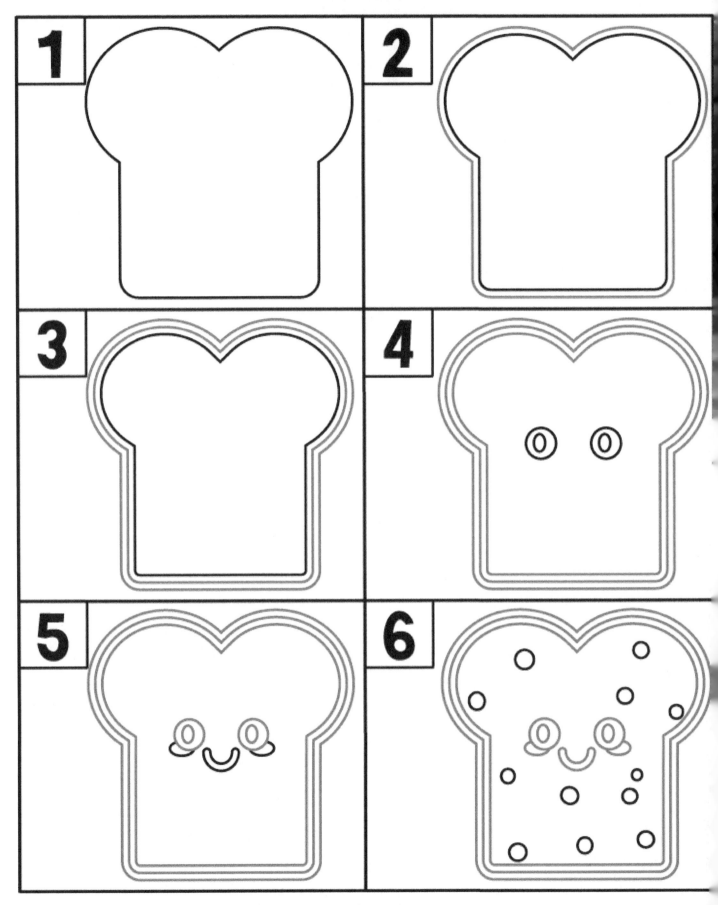

# PRACTICE HERE!

# SHARK

# PRACTICE HERE!

# COFFEE CUPS

# PRACTICE HERE!

# ICE CREAM

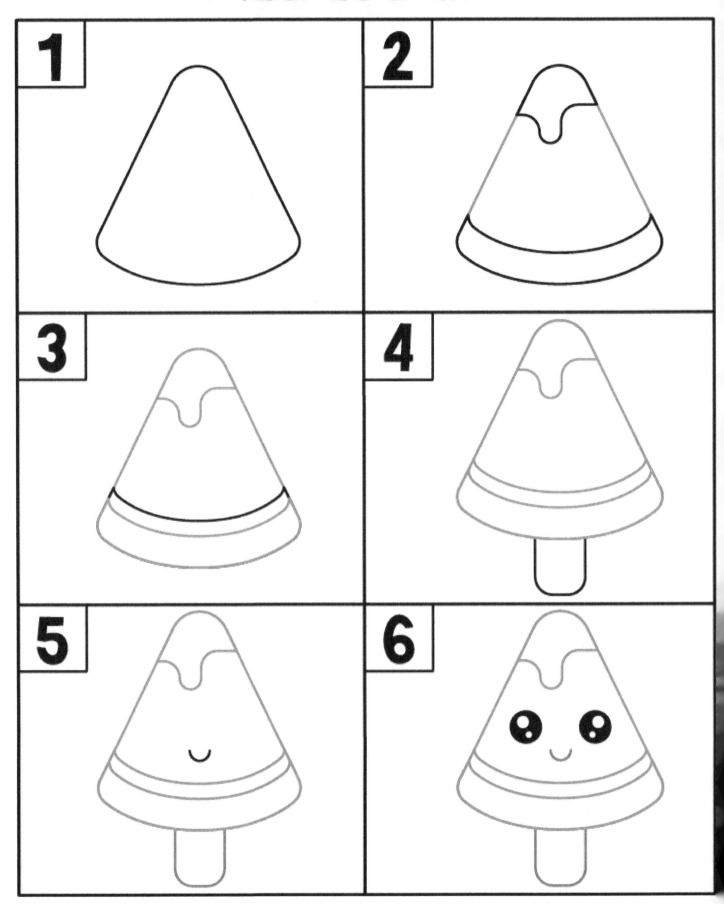

# PRACTICE HERE!

# CACTUS

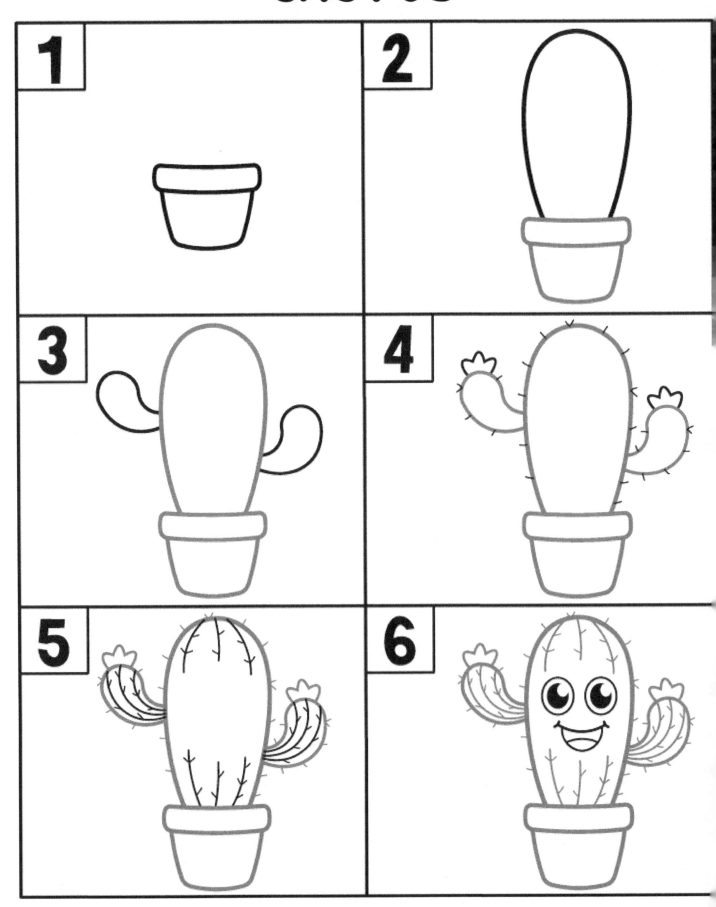

# PRACTICE HERE!

# TELEPHONE

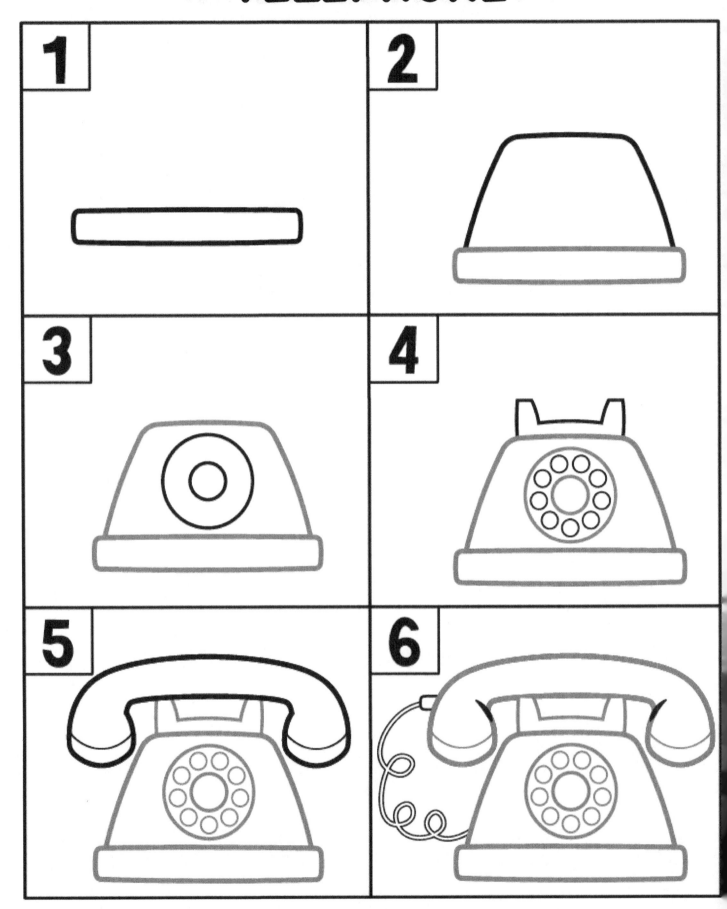

# PRACTICE HERE!

# DOG HOUSE

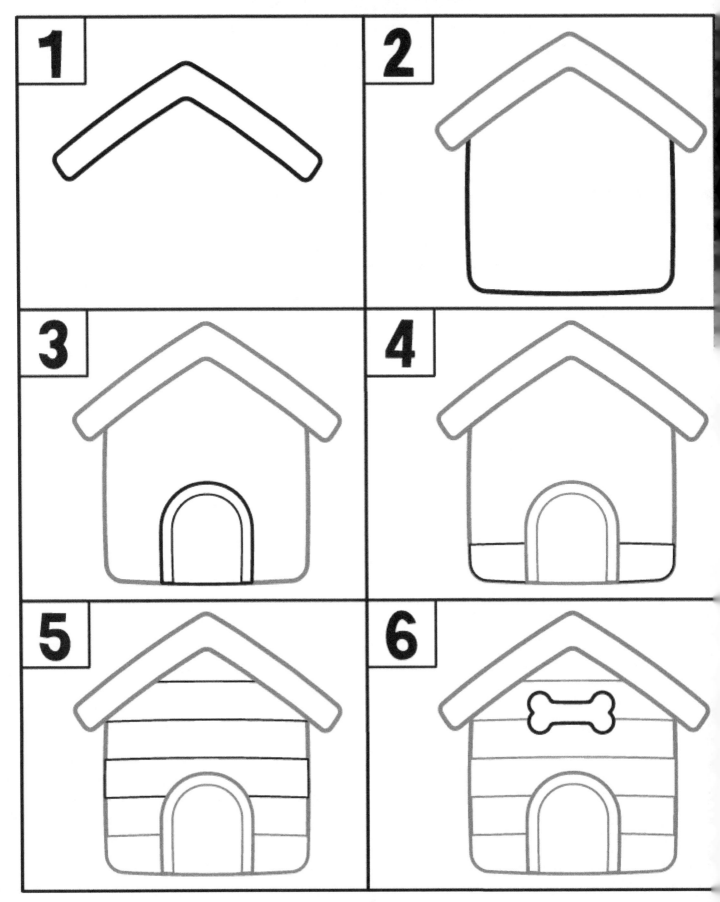

# PRACTICE HERE!

# BIRD HOUSE

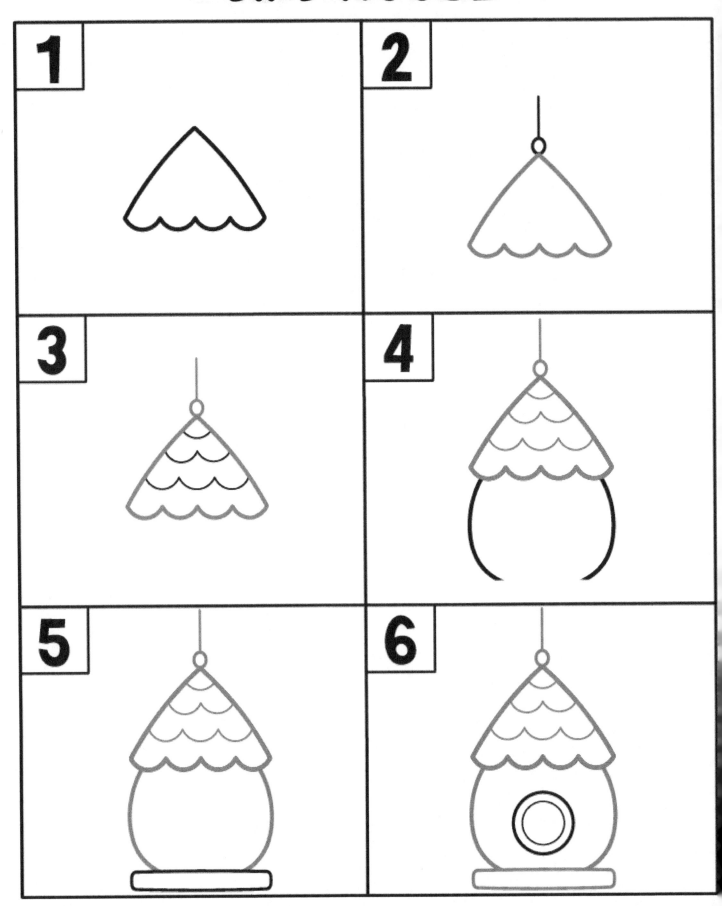

# PRACTICE HERE!

# BUTTERFLY

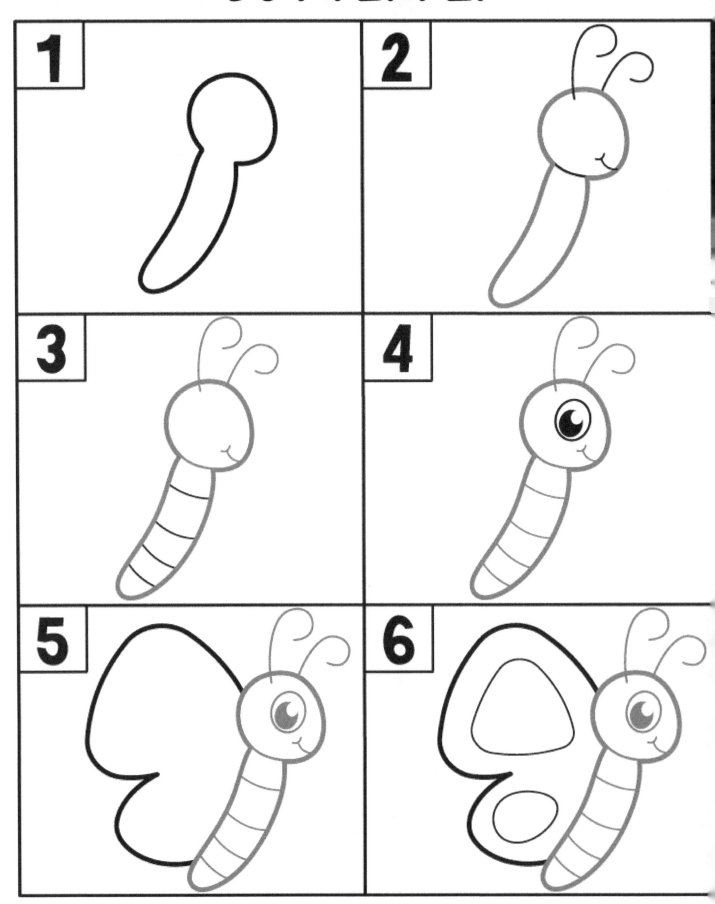

# PRACTICE HERE!

# CAKE

# PRACTICE HERE!

# CROWN

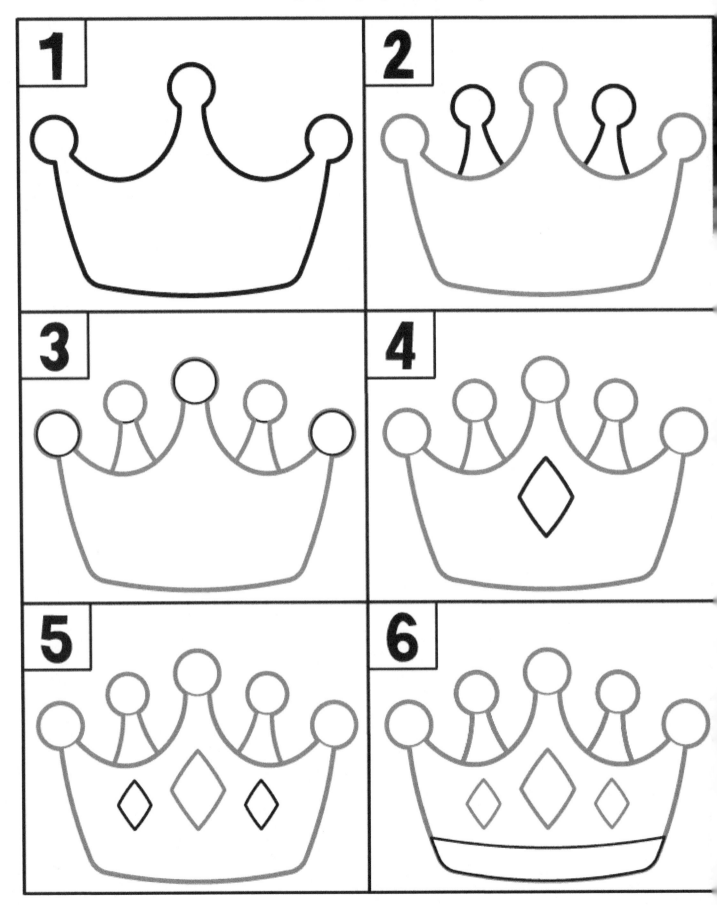

# PRACTICE HERE!

# MOON

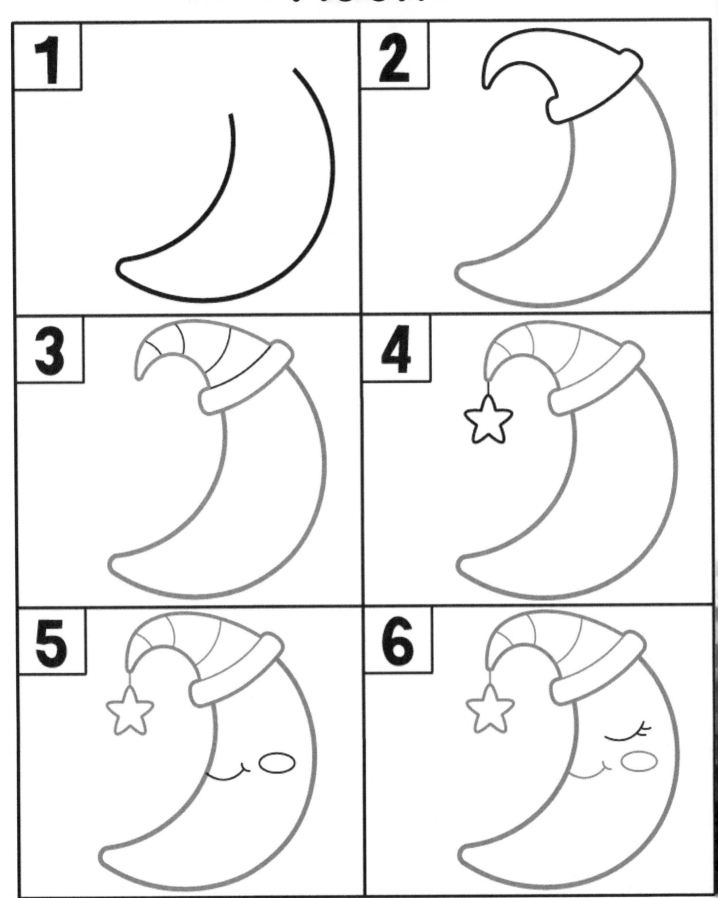

# PRACTICE HERE!

# BOAT

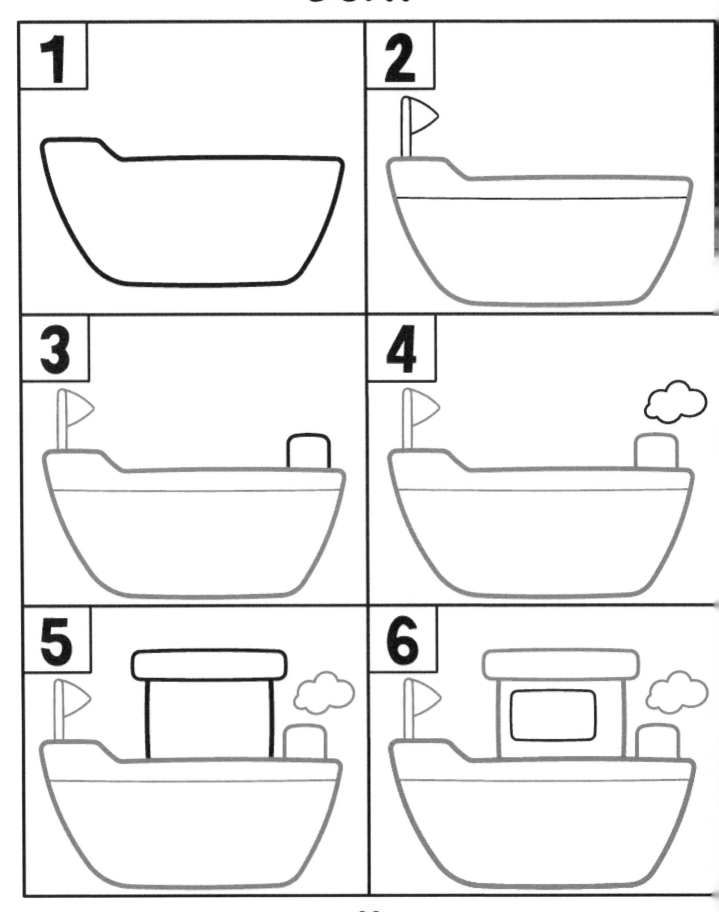

# PRACTICE HERE!

# CAR

# PRACTICE HERE!

# FISH

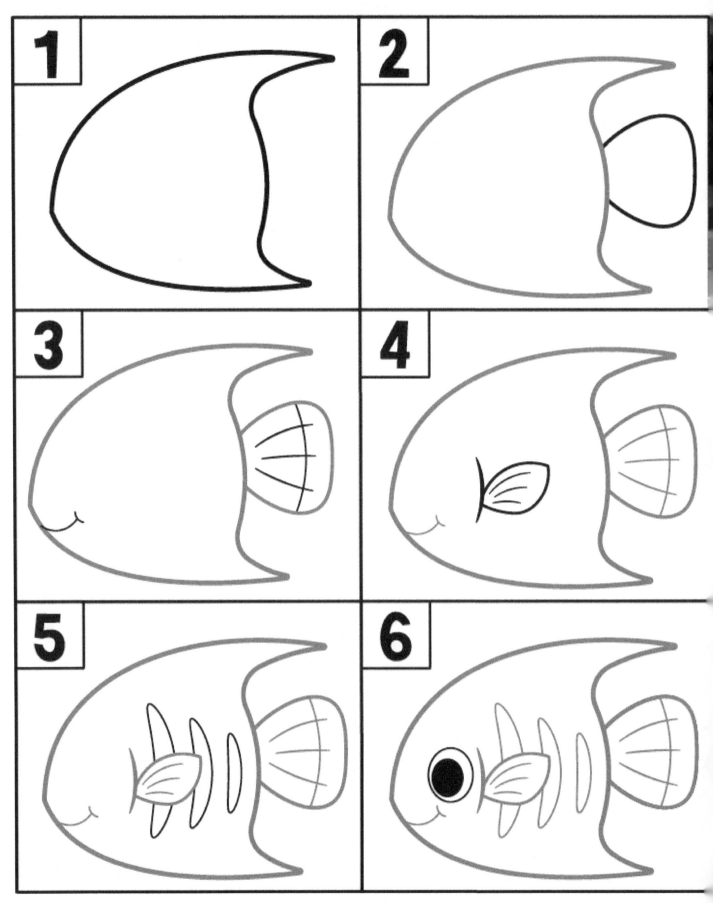

# PRACTICE HERE!

# BAG

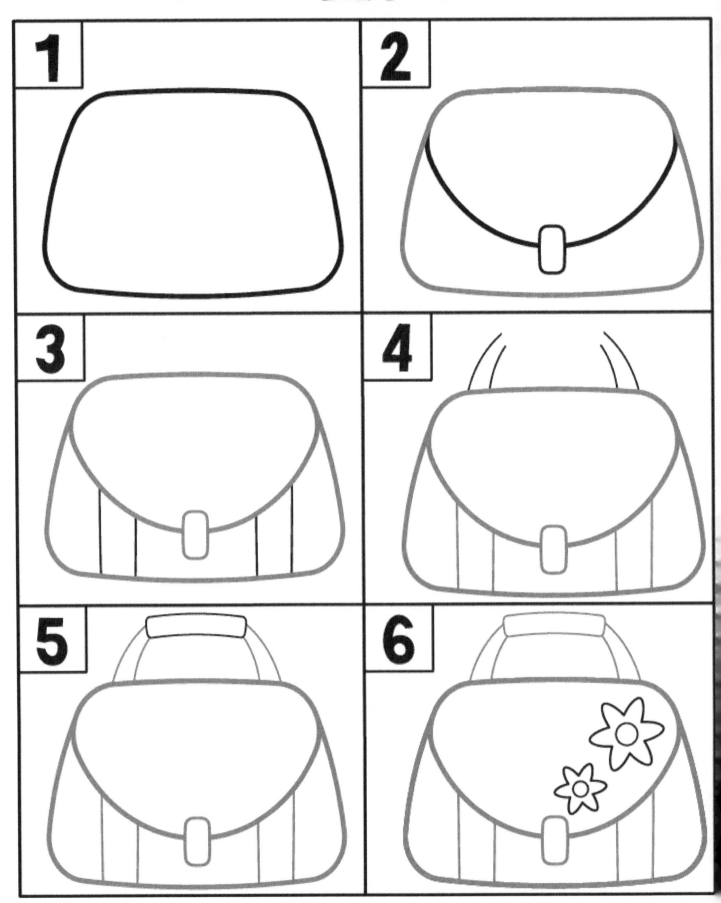

# PRACTICE HERE!

Made in the USA
Monee, IL
18 December 2024

74579527R00059